HOW TO WRITE YOUR STORY OF SUCCESS TO IMPACT THE WORLD

A Story Starter Guide
to Write Your Business or Personal Stories,
Goals and Achievements

MELANIE JOHNSON AND JENN FOSTER

How To Write Your Story of Success to Impact the World

A Story Starter Guide
to Write Your Business or Personal
Stories, Goals, and Achievements

By Melanie Johnson & Jenn Foster

How To Write Your Story of Success to Impact the World

2nd Edition
©2016, 2022 Elite Online Publishing

63 East 11400 South
Suite #230
Sandy, UT 84070
EliteOnlinePublishiing.com

ISBN: 978-1-956642-83-4 (eBook)
ISBN: 978-1-956642-84-1 (Paperback)
ISBN:978-1-956642-80-3 (Hardback)

LAN005060
LAN002000

DEDICATION

To our children! You inspire us every day! We are very proud of your accomplishments and success!

Check out our Free Bonus

Learn how to write your book with our free

guide, 9 Way to Write Your Book Fast

EliteOnlinePublishing.com/9-ways-to-write-a-book-fast

Also visit BestsellerSolutions.com

TABLE OF CONTENTS

ACKNOWLEDGMENTS

Our Kids, Nathan & Justice, for always pushing me and encouraging to do more and be better and keeping me on my toes!! I'm thankful every day that you are my sons.

Bailey, Carson & Brendan, for your patience and support for my business. You help me understand the meaning of life! I feel so blessed to have you all in my life.

Our Families, for all the support, love and standing by us through thick and thin.

Mike Koenigs, thank you for inspiring us to become authors and start our publishing business.

Chris & Pam Hendrickson, thanks for all your motivational videos and products. We love seeing you speak on stage!

Paul Colligan, thank you for inspiring and encouraging us to be brave enough to start our own podcast.

Darren Hardy, thank you for your daily inspirational emails. You push us to do better and better each day.

Tony Robbins, thank you for giving us strategies to make life easier.

And everyone else we may have forgotten to give thanks and praise to. We Thank you Very Much!

INTRODUCTION

"If my doctor told me I had only 6 months to live, I'd type a little faster."

– Isaac Asimov

If you have wanted to write a book of your life's journey, you have come to the right place. Did you know that 80% of people want to write a book and become an Author? But only 1% actually do it. This writing formula has had success year after year, book after book, when YOU IMPLEMENT. Get the results you want. The key is to IMPLEMENT!

Learn the single most powerful way to tell your life story and leave a legacy, for your family and friends. You will be leaving a slice of history by sharing your personal journey. The **"Success Story Starter"** will turn your stories and memories into a book.

Turn your ideas into a book within 60 days. When you read through this story starter guide, you will see how easy it is. You're going to see and know that by using our story starter questions, you will be able to do it! You may say, "But I'm not a writer."

WHAT IF I CAN'T WRITE?

You can be an author without having to be a writer. The big important idea behind this is pretty simple.

Here are some of the books that were written using this writing formula.

- ***Life Legacy Challenge***
- ***Books To Bucks***
- ***Podcast Authorized***
- ***Enthusiastic YOU!***
- ***Stand Apart - 5 Secrets to Marketing Your Business Online***

There are over 400 authors who have used similar tools and systems. Some of these authors had never written a book before and don't like to write. It's time to put the story of your life into a book to share for lifetimes to come.

You may be saying,

"I have a bunch of notes and journals and I just don't know how to put it all together!" Have you started writing a book and are stuck?

Continue reading and get your book together quickly, using the tools and strategies in this book. You will have your book published for years to come and be proud of it.

The First Step

Follow through the process in this story starter guide and get ready to implement. Take the first step: Pick a date right now to have your book written and released. Make a commitment. Once you have your date, share it. Share it on social media, with family or friends or even with one single person that will be an accountability partner for you.

Check out Melanie Johnson's TEDx Talk on YouTube. Search "Leaving a Legacy - The Time is Now" (https://youtu.be/aXyLNrnl7OE)

How to Write Without Being a Writer

Here are five ways to write a book without being a writer:

1. Talk your book instead of write your book. You can use the app "Evernote" or "Otter" to talk your story and the app will transcribe it as you go.

2. You can talk into your phone on "Notes" and it will transcribe it for you.

3. You can video yourself using your phone and a selfie stick and have it transcribed.

4. You can have someone interview you on video using your phone, camera or Zoom and have it transcribed.

5. You can hire a ghostwriter to go over the questions with you and write it all down.

TIPS:

- When using Evernote or Notes, you may have to talk slower and more precise, so it will stay up with you. We all tend to talk really fast, so you may have to slow down.

- The cool thing about video is that you can save it for later and upload it to YouTube. You can share it privately to just family and friends or you can share it to the whole world.

- Here are some websites we recommend to find a transcriber:

Upwork.com

fiverr.com

Question & Answer

This book is full of questions to get you thinking about the stories in your life. To open up your mind about your business or personal goals and achievements. Share your success with the world. But before you dive in and answer the questions, it's time to get your mindset ready and your brain turned on!

Now it's time to jump in and start your story. In the following chapters you will uncover answers to some of the best moments and memories of your childhood, teen years, young and mature adulthood up until the present. You will laugh and cry as you write or tell the stories that are special to you and made you who you are. It may trigger emotions you haven't felt in a long time, recalling a person you haven't thought of in years. Take the opportunity to reach out to them and remember old times and renew your friendship. This book is about your story but it's so much more than that. It's capturing your legacy and taking you through time. It would be great to sit around the family room with your children and grandchildren answering the questions. You may even consider doing the book as a fun party with your siblings or best friends all answering the questions together. Think about maybe recording it on otter.ai or zoom.

Tips:

- The book is in order of the timeline of your life, but feel free to do it the order that feels the most comfortable for you. If you are like me, you may jump around answering questions from different chapters during the same session.

- Don't feel overwhelmed that you have to finish the book all at one sitting. A couple great strategies are to answer a couple questions each morning to start your day or at the end of the day before you go to bed.

- When answering the questions think of Why you did it, When and how did you do it, Specific ways it has changed your life. Give as much detail as you can remember. So the reader can feel like they were there. For example, what was the weather like that day, what were your surroundings, the smell in the air, what your wore. Etc

- Be vulnerable. When you let yourself be vulnerable and transparent, something magical happens. "Vulnerability is a powerful thing in storytelling because it creates a human connection unlike anything else." You will not just be telling your story but creating a very personal and memorable connection with your reader. Tell your most important stories, the ones that touched your life and will touch the lives of your readers.

- Most of all have fun! Laugh, cry, ponder and reflect. Enjoy the journey whether you write it cozied up in your favorite chair or with a bunch of your family and friends.

GET YOUR HEAD IN THE GAME

DECLARE YOURSELF A WRITER - The words "I am" are very powerful. State it as a fact. Act like a writer, talk like a writer and start writing. Remember you become what you focus on.

BE OPEN - Allow yourself to be open to getting out of your comfort zone, accepting all forms of criticism, and overcoming your fears and inhibitions. Be Vulnerable. Here is a great TED talk on being vulnerable by Brene Brown.

https://youtu.be/iCvmsMzlF7o

EVERYDAY- Do something that moves you toward your goal of getting your book done everyday. It may not even be writing. You may research or observe something or take a few notes. It's the compound effect. It all adds up.

KNOW YOUR WHY- You have to know the reason why you are writing your book. What is your purpose? What do you want the outcome to be? How do you want your readers to feel after they read your book? What lessons, benefits or insights will they gain?

VISUALIZE- Picture how you will feel once you have told your story. Imagine what it's like to have completed sharing your legacy, story, knowledge and wisdom. Visualize how others will react once they know you have written a book. Visualize how the readers will feel and their expressions after they have read your book.

PLACES- Pick a special place to write or record your book. It can be a place that is special to you or that is quiet, where you can focus.

SET A DEADLINE- We challenged you in the paragraph above to set a date and share it with others. Most people work best with a deadline, so set your date and make it happen.

NEVER GIVE UP- If for some reason you miss

your deadline or you are still sitting with this workbook on your desk and you haven't implemented, don't beat yourself up, just try again. Today is a new day and the perfect day to get started.

Melanie Johnson & Jenn Foster

MINDSET MAKEOVER

HAPPY DAYS ARE HERE AGAIN!

Here are some great ways to get in a positive mindset before you write your book. Practice all or some of these. Not only will they put you in a great mood to write your book, they will improve your everyday life. Happiness is a choice, choose it every day!

Gratitude- When you feel there should be more to life, take an inventory of what you already have. Your health, family, friends, a place to live, clothes to wear, food to eat, your

17

skills and your dreams.

Giving- This makes us happier and healthier and it creates stronger connections between people. You can give your time, your ideas and your smile.

Exercising- Take care of your body; it's the only one you've got. The body and mind are connected. Being active makes us happier, improves our mood, helps us sleep better and gives us a strong energetic body.

Live in the Moment- Appreciate the world around you, even noticing the breeze rustling the leaves on a tree.

Grow- Keep learning new things. It gives us a sense of accomplishment and improves our wellbeing. It helps us stay curious and engaged.

Have Goals- This gives us something to look

forward to. Feeling good about our future is important for happiness. Goals excite us and motivate us. They give us direction.

Emotion- Research shows that regularly experiencing joy, gratitude, contentment, inspiration and pride creates an upward momentum in our spirit.

Acceptance- Love who you are. Be kind to yourself. Don't dwell on who you are not or compare yourself to others. We each have our unique gifts and talents and we should celebrate each other.

Purpose and Meaning- Be a part of something bigger. Leave a legacy and tell your story. People who have meaning and purpose in their lives are happier and live longer.

Motivation- Find your "Why". It could be a

goal, something you love, something you hate, or something you are passionate about.

Journaling- This releases the thoughts from the day or week. This helps us reflect and release everything that is rattling around in our head and put it down on paper.

Gratitude Journal- Write down the 5-10 things you are grateful for each day. Oprah says doing this one thing will change your life.

Read or Listen to Something Inspiring- Fill your head with positive, healthy, energizing, thoughts. This is health food for the brain.

Meditate or Pray- Take some quiet time for your mind to be at peace and rest with your creator.

Do an Activity as a Family- This will bond you together and create a memory.

Perform Random Acts of Kindness- If you want something you should give it away and then it will come back to you. If you want love, give love; if you want a mentor, be a mentor.

Create a Vision Board- Fill this with pictures of goals you would like to achieve and experience. Examples are: vacations, cars, houses, and romance.

Wake Up to Happy Music- Why not start your day on a upbeat, happy note! Pick music that has meaning to you and puts a smile on your face.

Dance Like Nobody's Watching- Really, turn on some music and go full-tilt crazy dancing. Watch how your mood will change.

Sweet Dreams- Think of a few things that really make you happy, or something you would like to experience that would put a smile on your face before you go to bed. You are programming your mind for what you want to dream about. People wake up happier when they have had a happy or positive dream the night before.

Breathe- Your body is primarily made up of water. It is 70% water and thrives on oxygen. Most of us don't breathe enough, especially if we don't do a great cardio workout. When we are stressed we tend to breathe shallowly. If you are like me, you hold your breath when stressing about things. Here is a quick tip. Take 10 deep breaths in for 4 seconds, holding each one for 4 seconds, then breath out for 6 seconds. Do this 3 times a day. Do it in the morning, in your car, while you are walking the dog, and lying in bed before you go to sleep. You will have more energy and be more relaxed and your mind will think more clearly.

Eat Well- Water, water, water! 70% of your diet should contain water rich foods. That means fruits and vegetables. Try this exercise; write down what you ate for the last 24 hours and see how much of it came from the earth versus pre-packaged.

You Are The Company You Keep- Stay away from the character Eeyore from Winnie The Pooh. Even though you're happy an energized attitude will be contiguous. People that live in the black abyss can suck you in. Limit your time from the terminal Eeyore types. Take inventory of the company you keep. Research shows you will start to take on the traits of the company you regularly keep. If they are always eating ice cream, before you know it, you will be eating ice cream with them. If they always use certain words or phrases, you will find that you start using some of the same words and phrases. (Just saying!)

Give a Compliment- It's amazing how someone's face will light up when you give them a sincere compliment. What happens afterward is that you get a warm fuzzy feeling inside knowing you have brightened someone's day.

Sleep Your Way to the Top- Getting enough sleep is imperative. Your brain doesn't function at full speed when you are sleep deprived. There is nothing pretty about being burnt out and exhausted.

Eat an Apple a Day- The saying is NOT eat a cookie a day. Think of the small stuff and the compound effect over time it will have. What if you did replace that cookie or cupcake with an apple or a piece of fruit? What would the result be after one week, one month, one year? It's the small things that will make a major difference in your life.

Smile, DAMN IT! - The best way to immediately reduce stress is to SMILE. Your body naturally relaxes when you smile. Wake up and smile before your feet hit the ground. When you first look into the mirror in the morning smile at yourself. Guess what? You'll be smiling right back at yourself. Isn't it nice to wake up to a happy face?

"Smile - It Increases Your Face Value!"
- Dolly Parton

Give Yourself a Hug- Literally wrap your arms around yourself and squeeze for a whole minute or so, take a few deep breaths and smile.

Own Happiness, Health and Productivity- Act Happy, talk like you're happy, walk like you're happy, think like you're happy, smile like you're happy, dress like you're happy. Put the actions behind your intention and they will become a reality.

P.S. I Love YOU!- First off, give yourself love. It's not enough to say it in your head. Stand in front of a mirror, look at yourself for about one minute or so in silence, gazing at all that you are and then say, "I Love you, I really love you." This practice has brought some people to tears the first time they do it. Now think of the people you love in your life and mentally send love to them. Then visualize how they will respond and look at you when they feel you love them. Now that's a pretty picture!

"We all have a life story and a message that can inspire others to live a better life or run a better business. Why not use that story and message to serve others?"

-Brendon Burchard

GOALS

"The future belongs to those who believe in the beauty of their dreams."

-Eleanor Roosevelt

1. Describe the event you took place in, or the goal you met.

_____

_____

_____

_____

_____

_____

_____

_____

_____

_____

_____

_____

_____

_____

_____

2. How were you introduced to this event/goal?

_____

_____

_____

_____

_____

_____

_____

_____

_____

_____

_____

_____

_____

_____

_____

3. What made you decide to set this goal or participate in the event?

_____

_____

_____

_____

_____

_____

_____

_____

_____

_____

_____

_____

_____

_____

_____

4. Once you thought of the prospect of accomplishing this goal, how long did it take you to really commit to it?

_____

_____

_____

_____

_____

_____

_____

_____

_____

_____

_____

_____

_____

_____

5. Did you write your goal down? Where? Describe how that made the goal more real.

_____

_____

_____

_____

_____

_____

_____

_____

_____

_____

_____

_____

_____

_____

_____

6. Did you share your goal with anybody? What was their response?

_____

_____

_____

_____

_____

_____

_____

_____

_____

_____

_____

_____

_____

_____

_____

7. Did you research the opportunity or just "dive in?"

_____

_____

_____

_____

_____

_____

_____

_____

_____

_____

_____

_____

_____

8. Describe your feeling before you started, as you were in the middle of the process and once you completed your goal.

_____

_____

_____

_____

_____

_____

_____

_____

_____

_____

_____

_____

_____

_____

9. Did you have to balance other goals or responsibilities to accomplish your goal?

_____

_____

_____

_____

_____

_____

_____

_____

_____

_____

_____

_____

_____

_____

10. Did you have a mentor that you looked to for success in helping achieve your goal?

_____

_____

_____

_____

_____

_____

_____

_____

_____

_____

_____

_____

_____

_____

Success Story Starter

MOTIVATION

"Never look where you're going...

always look where you want to go."

-Bob Ernst

1. What was your motivation for accomplishing this goal?

_____

_____

_____

_____

_____

_____

_____

_____

_____

_____

_____

_____

_____

_____

_____

2. How did you stay motivated?

_____

_____

_____

_____

_____

_____

_____

_____

_____

_____

_____

_____

_____

_____

_____

_____

3. Did your motivation stay the same or did it change? How?

_____

_____

_____

_____

_____

_____

_____

_____

_____

_____

_____

_____

_____

_____

_____

4. What did you learn about motivation during this experience?

_____

_____

_____

_____

_____

_____

_____

_____

_____

_____

_____

_____

_____

_____

5. Did you have doubts about accomplishing your goal or did you always feel confident? Did you feel you needed to look confident when you were doubtful?

----

6. How did you overcome discouragement?

_____

_____

_____

_____

_____

_____

_____

_____

_____

_____

_____

_____

_____

_____

_____

_____

7. Were others motivated by your actions?

_____

_____

_____

_____

_____

_____

_____

_____

_____

_____

_____

_____

_____

_____

_____

_____

8. Were others involved in your motivation?

_____

_____

_____

_____

_____

_____

_____

_____

_____

_____

_____

_____

_____

_____

_____

9. Did promises you made to yourself or others provide motivation? If so, what were those promises?

_____

_____

_____

_____

_____

_____

_____

_____

_____

_____

_____

_____

_____

_____

10. How would you define motivation?

_____

_____

_____

_____

_____

_____

_____

_____

_____

_____

_____

_____

_____

_____

_____

Success Story Starter

PLANNING

"Whether you think you can or think you can't, you're probably right."

-Henry Ford

1. Did you have a plan for accomplishing your goal?

_____

_____

_____

_____

_____

_____

_____

_____

_____

_____

_____

_____

_____

_____

2. If so, describe the plan in detail.

_____

_____

_____

_____

_____

_____

_____

_____

_____

_____

_____

_____

_____

_____

_____

_____

3. Did you write your plan down or share it with someone?

_____

_____

_____

_____

_____

_____

_____

_____

_____

_____

_____

_____

_____

_____

_____

4. Did you keep track of your plan on a chart or track your progress in some other way?

_____

_____

_____

_____

_____

_____

_____

_____

_____

_____

_____

_____

_____

_____

_____

5. Did your plan change during the process?

_____

_____

_____

_____

_____

_____

_____

_____

_____

_____

_____

_____

_____

_____

_____

_____

_____

_____

6. If so, how? Why?

_____

_____

_____

_____

_____

_____

_____

_____

_____

_____

_____

_____

_____

_____

_____

7. Did you have help creating your plan?

_____

_____

_____

_____

_____

_____

_____

_____

_____

_____

_____

_____

_____

_____

_____

_____

8. Looking back, what were the key parts of the plan that contributed most of your success or failure.

_____

_____

_____

_____

_____

_____

_____

_____

_____

_____

_____

_____

_____

_____

_____

9. Would you have been successful if you did not develop a plan?

_____

_____

_____

_____

_____

_____

_____

_____

_____

_____

_____

_____

_____

_____

_____

10. Was planning easy for you? Did your plan help keep you on course? Did you refer to your plan often?

_____

_____

_____

_____

_____

_____

_____

_____

_____

_____

_____

_____

_____

_____

_____

Success Story Starter

LESSONS

"The very difficulty of a problem evokes abilities or talents which would otherwise, in happy times, never emerge to shine."

-Horace

1. What lessons did you learn while working on your goal?

_____

_____

_____

_____

_____

_____

_____

_____

_____

_____

_____

_____

_____

_____

2. How was your character developed while working toward your goal?

_____

_____

_____

_____

_____

_____

_____

_____

_____

_____

_____

_____

_____

_____

3. What did you learn about yourself?

_____

_____

_____

_____

_____

_____

_____

_____

_____

_____

_____

_____

_____

_____

_____

_____

4. What did you learn about others?

_____

_____

_____

_____

_____

_____

_____

_____

_____

_____

_____

_____

_____

_____

_____

_____

_____

5. Would you try to accomplish this endeavor again? Why?

_____

_____

_____

_____

_____

_____

_____

_____

_____

_____

_____

_____

_____

_____

_____

6. Was there a time you felt like giving up? What made you change your mind?

_____

_____

_____

_____

_____

_____

_____

_____

_____

_____

_____

_____

_____

_____

_____

7. What encouragement would you give others who wanted to try the same thing?

_____

_____

_____

_____

_____

_____

_____

_____

_____

_____

_____

_____

_____

_____

_____

8. Do you have any regrets about a direction you took? Would you do anything differently?

_____

_____

_____

_____

_____

_____

_____

_____

_____

_____

_____

_____

_____

_____

9. What was your proudest moment during your experience?

_____

_____

_____

_____

_____

_____

_____

_____

_____

_____

_____

_____

_____

_____

_____

10. Was there something that you didn't want to do, but had to do it anyway? How did it turn out?

_____

_____

_____

_____

_____

_____

_____

_____

_____

_____

_____

_____

_____

_____

Success Story Starter

WHO HELPED MAKE IT HAPPEN

"Interdependence is and ought to be as much the ideal of man as self-sufficiency. Man is a social being."

- Mahatma Gandhi

1. Who helped you accomplish your goal?

_____

_____

_____

_____

_____

_____

_____

_____

_____

_____

_____

_____

_____

_____

_____

_____

2. Who provided support for you? Was their support "active" or "passive"?

_____

_____

_____

_____

_____

_____

_____

_____

_____

_____

_____

_____

_____

_____

_____

3. What did they do to help you succeed?

_____

_____

_____

_____

_____

_____

_____

_____

_____

_____

_____

_____

_____

_____

_____

4. Did others participate in the event or process?

_____

_____

_____

_____

_____

_____

_____

_____

_____

_____

_____

_____

_____

_____

_____

5. If so, who were they? How did they participate?

_____

_____

_____

_____

_____

_____

_____

_____

_____

_____

_____

_____

_____

_____

_____

6. Did anyone discourage or interfere with your plans?

_____

_____

_____

_____

_____

_____

_____

_____

_____

_____

_____

_____

_____

_____

_____

_____

7. What did you learn about the importance of other people in meeting your goals?

_____

_____

_____

_____

_____

_____

_____

_____

_____

_____

_____

_____

_____

_____

8. Did you feel intimidated by sharing your goals with those close to you?

_____

_____

_____

_____

_____

_____

_____

_____

_____

_____

_____

_____

_____

_____

_____

9. How did your relationships improve as you allowed people close to you to support your experiences?

_____

_____

_____

_____

_____

_____

_____

_____

_____

_____

_____

_____

_____

_____

10. Was anyone envious of your success?

_____

_____

_____

_____

_____

_____

_____

_____

_____

_____

_____

_____

_____

_____

_____

_____

Success Story Starter

What's Next

Congratulations! If you are on this page that means you have finished your questions and your book. Way to go! You are now part of the 1% that write and finish a book. Now you can decide to share it with the world or just keep it private for you family and personal friends. If you listened to Melanie's TEDx talk, you know we are big on sharing stories, knowledge, and wisdom with the world. And more often than not, once people know that you have written a book, they will all want a copy. The easiest way to do that is to make it available on Amazon. An author we worked with at first just wanted to print 20 copies, then when the world got out, friends and family from all over the country wanted a copy. We ended up putting it for sale on Amazon and it sells copies every month. The other choice is to print copies at a local printer and mail them out yourself to all those clamoring to get a copy.

Before you can print the book, there still is a little bit of work to do. You'll want to have a beautiful book cover design. We use a team of graphic artists for our clients, but you can find book cover designers on Fiverr.com or Upwork. You can hire a book formatter there too. Formatting is taking your word document and turning it into a professional ready for print, pdf document.

Before you send it to the formatter have it looked over by either a professional editor or have someone you trust edit it.

Now it's time to publish your book. You may be saying I don't have the slightest idea to do that. We are here to help. We have a digital video training course for publishing, or you can hire us one on one.

Now is the time to share your life story and share your legacy to your prosperity and to the world.

"I think I did pretty well, considering I started out with nothing but a bunch of blank paper." – Steve Martin

ABOUT THE AUTHORS

Melanie Churella Johnson

Melanie is a WSJ/USA Today bestselling author and 15x Amazon bestseller. She launched, owned, and operated a $100 million media company with TV stations in Houston and Dallas Texas: Houston (Channel 51) and Dallas (Channel 55). Melanie started her career as a News Anchor in Detroit at Channel 20 after she won the title of Miss Michigan and was first runner up to Miss

America. Melanie has a background in Media, Marketing, Public Relations and Advertising. She has been in front of, as well as behind the camera. She was a News Anchor, Producer, Writer, Public Relations, Promotions, TV ad sales, Programming negotiations and Financial Strategist. She has done business with Warner Brothers, Disney, King World and MGM Studios. In addition to creating and developing successful businesses she has created award winner advertising campaigns.

Melanie is the CEO and co-owner of Elite Online Publishing. They publish, market and promote nonfiction books for business owners and athletes to create expert authority status for marketing impact and influence. She is passionate about sharing people's stories that educate, motivate and inspire. She is honored to work one on one with their authors to create the best strategies for their book creation, marketing, and social media.

Melanie was honored to be a TEDx speaker in Sugarland, Texas in 2016, where she spoke on the importance of leaving a legacy. She is the co-host of the Elite Expert Insider podcast on iTunes and Stitcher Radio and has a YouTube channel.

She got her feet wet in the luxury building and design industry when she was the general contractor and developer for her personal 25,000 square foot home known as "The Houston Mansion" and her 13,000 square foot summer home in Petoskey, Michigan "The Walloon Lake House." During the economic downturn, Melanie turned both of these properties into successful Luxury Vacation and Event Rental Properties and continues to invest and develop real estate.

She is the CEO of Charity Auction Consignments. Melanie graciously donates her Villa in the Dominican Republic along with her other properties to help raise money for children's issues, health, education, and animals. She works with numerous charities including Texas Children's Hospital, Citizens for Animal Protection, Fanatical Change Foundation, Just Like My Child Foundation and a variety of private schools.

Melanie graduated from Michigan State University with a degree in communications and was the first girl to receive a varsity letter in a boys sport in the state of Michigan. She lives in Houston, Texas and is originally from Michigan. She is enjoying raising her two sons, who keep her motivated and young. She loves the beach, traveling and spending time with her family.

Follow Melanie at:

AuthorMelanieJohnson.com

Facebook.com/authormelaniejohnson

Instagram.com/melaniecjohnson

LinkedIn.com/in/melaniejohnson-eop

Eliteonlinepublishing.com

JENN FOSTER

Jenn is a Wall Street Journal, USA Today and International bestselling author. She is the owner of Elite Online Publishing and Biz Social Marketing Agency. Companies dedicated to helping business owners of all sizes thrive in today's highly technical world of product and service promotion. Jenn owned and operated a successful local chain of retail stores, where she honed her online marketing skills. From local brick and mortar stores to online entities, to large international corporations, Jenn's years of experience and expertise have now helped hundreds of businesses become front page news on major search engines. She is dedicated to helping businesses use powerful new online and mobile marketing platforms to get visibility, traffic, leads, customers and raving fans. She is passionate about helping busy entrepreneurs, business leaders, and professionals to create, publish, and market their book, to build their business and brand. She encourages new authors to share their stories, knowledge and expertise to help others. With her marketing and digital background, Jenn uses the best strategies for her client's books to boost their sales and marketing platforms and helps them achieve #1 bestselling status.

A graduate of Utah State University, Jenn is an award winning web designer, author and sought after speaker. She has been a featured panelist and speaker at events with experts like Loral Langemier, Lisa Sasevich, Mike Koenigs, Ed Rush and more. Jenn has been named one of America's Premier Experts® and is highlighted in the Dan Kennedy Book, **Stand Apart**. Jenn Foster was recently named one of "Utah's Thought Leaders" in the book **Innovate Utah** by Global Village. Jenn is the co-host of Elite Expert Insider Podcast on iTunes and Spotify.

Coming from a family of successful entrepreneurs, her Grandfather started the Maverik Country Stores oil and gas station chain which is still thriving today. Jenn grew up around successful businesses and understands from the ground up what it takes to create, run and promote winning companies. Combining her education, knowledge and life-long experience, today Jenn teaches people and businesses globally how they can get found in today's virtual world, how they can engage prospects on their terms and how to continue to connect and follow up with prospects to convert them to customers.

Jenn is a single Mom who loves spending time with her three children, traveling, and experiencing the great outdoors.

Follow Jenn Foster:

AuthorJennFoster.com

Eliteonlinepublishing.com

Facebook.com/authorjennfoster

Instagram.com/jennfosterchic

LinkedIn.com/in/jennfosterseo

ELITE
ONLINE
PUBLISHING

About Elite Online Publishing

We believe you have a story to tell, and we know that the lives of your readers will be vastly improved from learning from your expertise.

That's why we help authors write, market, and publish a book they can be proud of. With our full-service publishing packages, we help you build your book from start to finish, develop your personal brand that speaks to your expertise, then create an insatiable buzz that launches you to Bestseller status.

Our greatest pride comes from our ability to turn ordinary business leaders with little to no writing experience into accomplished authors who top the charts and become instant authorities. Many of our authors have beat out books published by authors like Tina Fey, Tim Ferris, and Robin Williams. We help authors find their voice through writing workshops, masterclasses, and content creation of digital courses. Our collaborations last long past launch day, all our authors are part of the Elite Online Publishing family.

Whether you want to publish an eBook, paperback, hardback, or audiobook we'll ensure your book reaches the top of the bestseller list. Elite Online Publishing's services also include video production,

Amazon author page design, social media posting, website design, and management to ensure your success grows. With us, you'll get individualized assistance and hands-on support to craft the story you were meant to share.

When we're not publishing chart-topping books, founders and owners Melanie Johnson and Jenn Foster interview inspirational speakers and entrepreneurs on Elite Publishing's podcast, *Elite Expert Insider.*

To get your book published visit

EliteOnlinePublishing.com

Subscribe to our Podcast on iTunes or anywhere you listen to podcasts - Look for

Elite Expert Insider. **Elite.libsyn.com**

Subscribe to our YouTube Channel

YouTube.com/eliteonlinepublishing1

Check out our Free Bonus

Learn how to write your book with our free

guide, 9 Way to Write Your Book Fast

EliteOnlinePublishing.com/9-ways-to-write-a-book-fast

Also visit BestsellerSolutions.com

www.ingramcontent.com/pod-product-compliance
Lightning Source LLC
Chambersburg PA
CBHW071203120626
46546CB00006B/2397